A-Z VICTORY

Alphabet Power Affirmations

TANNER HEIL

BALBOA.PRESS

A DIVISION OF HAY HOUSE

Balboa Press books may be ordered through booksellers or by contacting:

Balboa Press
A Division of Hay House
1663 Liberty Drive
Bloomington, IN 47403
www.balboapress.com
844-682-1282

Print information available on the last page.

ISBN: 978-1-9822-7970-7 (sc)
ISBN: 978-1-9822-7972-1 (hc)
ISBN: 978-1-9822-7971-4 (e)

Library of Congress Control Number: 2022902079

Balboa Press rev. date: 02/23/2022

CONTENTS

DEDICATION

This is dedicated to my family. Both my immediate family and my fishing family. I am grateful for the tenacity and dedication, of the men and women in my life. This book wouldn't be possible without the leadership of strong, disciplined, and devoted individuals.

To my parents Brad and Denise, you raised me well, and I am proud to be your son. Thank you so much for the sacrifices you've made to support me. Every step from infant to an adult, I take this moment to appreciate your love and unconditional support.

I am grateful for the people I am surrounded with in the fishing industry. Working from dusk to dawn and every opportunity between, I have learned earnest persistence. To Adamant Fisheries, thank you for sparking the flame within and teaching me self-belief. I am forever grateful for learning from you to persist through adversity. To the Nelson family, thank you for teaching me to hustle and earn my way. You have showed me what it takes to be ahead of the game, and to be ready when the moment of opportunity arrives. From land I have learned what is stable, from the sea I have learned to embrace the ferocious waves of life.

This book is dedicated to my friends and family who have guided me home. I feel blessed to have access to healthy lifestyle choices that have shaped my reality. This is dedicated to my family who make the journey possible.

ABOUT THE BOOK

Welcome to the A-Z Victory! This is an affirmation dictionary in alphabetical order! A-Z Victory is designed to inspire and promote I am sentences. I am sentences are a form of self-talk. Self-talk has been known as a phycological technique that can be used by anyone. Regardless of age, we can all practice positive self-talk to support the mind, body, and spirit. The mind being the powerhouse to consciousness. Regardless of personal endeavor, we each share the experience of adversity! Adversity is inevitable. And through adversity of life, one needs fortitude to persevere!

Is the bully causing self-doubt? Is your boss killing your vibe? A-Z Victory is a guiding light. Let the words of A-Z Victory lighten the negative feedback loop within our minds. Taking ownership of what we tell ourselves mentally is a fast route to changing our perspectives. All it takes is a shift in perspective to create a positive effect in our personal reality. A-Z Victory is a dictionary of powerful affirmations that can support and encourage ownership. Ownership of a healthy mind, body, and spirit! The act of ownership with our personal narrative is free. You have the power and choice to choose what you think! A-Z Victory can be used to promote self-love. Self-love is a form of personal self-care which leads to success in life. May this empower you to be sovereign and self-loving.

A-Z Victory is a concentrated dictionary of words in alphabetic order that promote positive self-talk. The power of I am is infinite! This publication is designed to promote creative exploration. A-Z Victory is intended to create and cultivate the best possible I am sentences for YOU! Use I am sentences that encourage and empower yourself. Created for any individual who is exploring the power and application of positive and encouraging self-talk. A-Z victory is a guide to inspire and promote I am sentences that work best for the reader. We are all unique and different in our own ways, so I offer you the opportunity to engage and make it fun!

AFFIRMATION, AFFIRMATION, AFFIRMATION!

I was taught from a young age to listen to my intuition, follow my heart, and trust my body. I've climbed mountains, skied marathons, endured storms on the ocean, and conquered the monsters from within. All stemming from the compounding effects of positive affirmation.

Every step throughout my life has been filled with trial and adversity. I have been fortunate having the opportunity to be surrounded by some truly fierce and tenacious leaders. Leaders who taught the importance of hard work and dedication. Through my work experience I have learned to hammer through the humps and leave nothing to chance. I have learned to persevere through cold miserable weather in wet clothes. I have learned to maintain relentless discipline through the entirety of a season. And most importantly I have learned to believe in myself. Despite fatigue, exhaustion, and drudgery. Hidden deep inside my core, is a habit of eternal self-belief.

Early on in my career, in the very beginning I was clean as a blank slate. An empty canvas, eager to be painted. I absorbed the wisdom of my teachers like a sponge. Listening to every comment, criticism, and complaint. I digested the information and stored the wisdom. All of it including the holler of excitement to the screams of anger of the day. I processed with discernment to understand each message. I felt as though some days I was the protégé and was overloaded with material. But still I received the message to persist and learn.

The most keystone moment of my career was after a hard day of work. A hard day of fishing. A day of true adversity. It was in the month of May when the winter ground is still hard and the snow is beginning to melt throughout western Alaska. It was a cold spring! We were anchored on the Nunavachak beach Southeast of Togiak village. This particular day It was so cold that the salt-water was freezing on deck. The wind was drawing so much heat from the exhaust stack that a 5-gallon bucket was tied to the tip to prevent the wind from sucking the heat right out! Regardless of the temperature we still had to go to work.

Coincidently the boat is named Adversity. We aboard, were participating in the cooperative harvest of herring for the valuable sac-roe they contain. On this specific day we had labored relentlessly in earnest battle. Battle with the elements, the ocean, and the hard-to-catch herring. Set after set we labored. After we had exhausted the time of the day, we motored toward anchorage so we could drop the anchor to rest. I was physically spent, and thankfully it was dinner time. As a member of the crew, at the end of every day my job was to clean up the deck, and get inside. All the while, my captain; man of honor and energy, was whipping together a meal. To my amazement, the table was set with perfectly cooked, moist, juicy, steaming red meat. In addition to separate pots of mashed potatoes, gravy, mixed vegetables, and a loaf of bread! I had learned to expect this kind of deliberate excellence but let me set a reference point. This was not how the rest of the fleet was eating. Most boats were most likely chewing on a chunk of over cooked meat and instant noodles. To say the least, I felt very lucky and privileged to be part of the operation. We all dished up and forked in. I devoured what I could knowing the energy was to be replenished. I ate as if I was the garbage disposal, but chewed in gratitude. The food was delicious, and I admired the effort, so I made a quick comment.

"Thanks, Eric!"

I remember thinking how in the world am I supposed to live up to this. Aspiring to one day be captain myself, this was a bar I felt was going to be impossible to live up to. All 4 of us finished eating, I cleared my throat and in a complimentary way asked the pivotal question.

"How do you do it?

With confidence he said,
"Affirmation, affirmation, affirmation!"

His response was unexpected. I was expecting a literal explanation of the preparation and cooking process. At the time, I was naive in age and ignorant to the truth. With a full belly and a body that was ready to rest, I acknowledged his statement and made my way to the sink to clean up. I scrubbed the pots and silverware as I pondered about these affirmations, affirmations, affirmations. My mind raced with curiosity.

What is an affirmation? Are affirmations important? How do I use one? Where do I find them? I retired to my bunk and made the promise to myself to pursue these "affirmations" once back home. The mission was set with intention to better myself. All with the hope to grow into the man I wished to become.

WHAT IS AN AFFIRMATION?

An affirmation is the action of affirming something. Specifically, we are affirming ourselves. We are declaring the facts. Affirmations are for affirming qualities of ourselves in our individual ways. We are declaring our top qualities! Affirmations are not for degrading ourselves or negative use. Our brains need love and affirmations are the love it understands. Affirmations are metaphorical nutrients as if we were watering our souls with words. Through affirmation we feed our internal fertile landscape with positive affirmation and soak up the nutrients.

When we complement our friends for their unique style, we are complimenting their style. When we affirm ourselves, we are affirming the qualities that we see in ourselves. A deliberate compliment, that is well deserved. Such as I am strong! Affirmations elevate perspective of value. Putting importance upon a specific quality, or characteristic. Affirmations could be thought of as compliments for ourselves. Affirmations are confirming these compliments to be true.

ARE AFFIRMATIONS IMPORTANT?

Phycology and self-help literature teach that self-help begins from within. Beginning with ourselves, we all have the ability to become aware of our own self-talk. This self-talk is fundamental in reshaping the internal landscape of the conscious mind. Affirmations are basic building blocks within the mind. Beginning within the mind, thoughts ripple outwards into life. Thoughts create the foundation for beliefs and beliefs become the structure of choice. These choices create the results of life.

Affirmations are simple truths. Simple truths that become the structures of belief. They hold real estate in our minds. This structure can be positive or negative depending on how we choose. The narrative we tell ourselves is the foundation of our thoughts, perspectives, beliefs. It is the architecture of our reality. The internal narrative we listen to or tell ourselves is the forerunner to how we act, choose and ultimately live. Fundamentally, the words we choose program our mental reality.

Mental health is a component to strong physical health. With building blocks one can climb the stair case to a full, and integrated healthy life. No matter what stage of existence, I am affirmations can be helpful in creating an excellent mindset. A-Z Victory is a supplement to kick start your self-love game!

This internal narrative is important in maintaining stable mental health. For the individual with stable mental health, doors of opportunity and abundance are opened. At this individual level, one who is mentally stable is able to interact and engage in society with intentional contribution. A-Z Victory promotes healthy mental health with emphasis on self-affirmation.

HOW DO I USE ONE?

Affirmations have infinite application. I can be serious, and state serious truths. I can be complimentary, and affirm myself with love. I can affirm my discipline and affirm my strengths. I can speak positively and support myself in healthy ways. I can pump myself up and fill my mental space with positivity.

Starting from when we wake up, we can practice self-love through affirmation. Looking in the mirror briefly or when I brush my teeth, I can reference these affirmations. Perhaps even before I rest, affirmations are a great tool to end the day. I use them to ground myself and find my center. I use them when I need a confidence boost before a meeting. I use affirmations while I train or workout. I use affirmations to start the day and I use them to end the day. Affirmations can be used anytime, anywhere.

Stepping into the transformative function of affirmation we capitalize on our self-love. We choose to act from a place of self-love. Self-love is taking responsibility and taking ownership of yourself. Beginning from the fundamental level of thought, affirmations are a building block to establishing a healthy relationship with ourselves. A-Z Victory promotes acting in conscious, intentional, self-loving ways.

We hold the power to shape the reality of which we believe about self-love. Some have described self-love/self-help as selfish or vain or an outlet of narcissism or conceit. I do not advocate for excessive pride in oneself. There is a dichotomy to this practice. There is a difference between arrogant egoic-self affirmation and humble self-loving affirmation. One fans the flames of arrogance and the latter nurtures the voice of the soul.

WHERE DO I FIND THEM?

A-Z Victory is an essential dictionary of affirmations. Descriptions that assist in positive self-affirmation. Some adjectives may not align with your situation so it is okay to not resonate with these words. Use what works for you! My intentions of this book are to guide individuals toward a full and integrated life of self-love.

Self-love can be a remedy to negative habits that are hard to curb. These could be issues relating to negative choices, actions, habits. Or as extreme as self-defeat, self-neglect, self-punishment just to list a few. Self-love is a modern approach to tackle destructive habits and promote self-love.

A-Z Victory is intended to guide the reader through the basics of positive self-talk. Designed with intentions to improve the individual personal narrative. Printed with space for the reader to customize and cultivate positive affirmation for themselves. Enjoy the alphabet of positive I am sentences!

HOW TO USE THIS BOOK?

As you open the A-Z Victory, in the upper left corner on the left-hand side you will see a letter of the alphabet. The heading of the page is consistent throughout the book with **I am...** This is to be read as the root before each successive word.

Listed below are corresponding alphabetic words. Listed below in bold to give the reader directional flow from the root I am. Each word has a dictionary definition next to it. You can read into these definitions to better understand each word.

After you have read through each letter, the right page is for you! As the reader you will see on the right side, there is space to write your own. Mark it up! Make it your own! Write out your I am sentences, ask questions, draw, pray, meditate, do anything to interact with these I am sentences!

Use this interactive publication as a resource to maximize your potential and support your performance throughout all walks of life. A-Z Victory is a resource to magnify positive self-love.

Be creative, have fun, and most importantly give yourself positive affirmation. After all that's what winners do!

Aa

I AM...

Awesome. Extremely impressive or daunting; inspiring great admiration, apprehension, or fear.

Alive. (Of a person, animal, or plant) living, not dead.

Assertive. Having or showing a confident and forceful personality.

Audacious. Showing a willingness to take surprisingly bold risks.

Aware. Knowledgeable or perceptive of a situation or fact.

Ambitious. Having or showing a strong desire and determination to succeed.

Attractive. Pleasing or appealing to the senses.

Aggressive. Pursuing one's aims and interests forcefully.

Action. The fact or process of doing something, typically to achieve an aim.

"Very little is needed to make a happy life; it is all within yourself, in your way of thinking."
Marcus Aurelius

AFFIRM YOUR I AM!

EXAMPLE: I am Ambitious!

"*All that we are is the result of what we have thought.*"

Buddha

Bb

I AM...

Bold. Showing an ability to take risks; confident and courageous.

Balanced. Taking everything into account; fairly judged or presented.

Badass. (Urban definition). Uncommon person of supreme style, radiates confidence in everything he/she does and fears nobody.

Bliss. Perfect happiness; great joy.

*"All of humanity's problems stem from man's
inability to sit quietly in a room alone."*
Blaise Pascal

STATE YOUR BEST QUALITIES!

EXAMPLE: I am balanced.

"Until you're ready to look foolish, you'll never have the possibility to be great."

Cher

Cc

I AM...

Consistent. Acting in the same way over time, especially so as to be fair or accurate.

Confident. Feeling or showing confidence in oneself; self-assured.

Classy. Stylish and sophisticated.

Champion. A person who has defeated or surpassed all rivals in a competition.

Courageous. Not deterred by danger or pain; brave.

Calm. Not showing or feeling nervousness, anger, or other strong emotions.

Clever. Quick to understand, learn, and devise or apply ideas; intelligent.

"Whatever you do, do with all your might." Cicero

CREATE YOUR OWN!

EXAMPLE: I am courageous!

"Your thoughts are architects of your destiny."

David D. McKay

Dd

I AM...

Decisive. Settling an issue; producing a definite result.

Dedicated. Devoted to a task or purpose; having single-minded loyalty or integrity.

Dependable. Trustworthy and reliable.

Determined. Having made a firm decision and being resolved not to change it.

Dynamic. Positive in attitude and full of energy and new ideas.

Disciplined. Showing a controlled form of behavior or way of working.

Doughty. Brave and persistent.

"Action may not always bring happiness; but
there is not happiness without action."
Benjamin Disrael

DO IT YOURSELF!

EXAMPLE: I am disciplined in my pursuit.

"You are now, and you do become, what you think about."

Earl Nightingale

I AM...

Energetic. Showing great activity or vitality.

Excellent. Extremely good; outstanding.

Excelsior. (Latin) Ever upward.

Earnest. Serious and sincere.

Engaging. Tending to draw favorable interest or attention; attractive.

Ecstasy. Experiencing overwhelming feelings of great happiness or joyful excitement.

"Timing is everything." Eric Rosvold

DESCRIBE YOUR INNER EXCELLENCE!

EXAMPLE: Every time I win, I feel inner ecstasy!

"When you come to the end
of your hope,
tie a knot and hang on."
Franklin D. Roosevelt

I AM...

Faithful. Loyal, constant, steadfast.

Fearless. Lacking fear.

Flexible. Ready and able to change to adapt to different circumstances.

Ferocious. Extreme in degree, power, or effect.

Fortunate. Favored by good luck or fortune; lucky.

Free will. The power of acting freely, with the ability to act at one's own discretion.

"There is more wisdom in your body than your deepest philosophy" Friedrich Nietzsche

HAVE FAITH AND GIVE IT A TRY!

EXAMPLE: I am flexible and fortunate!

"Remember even though you cannot scale the wall today doesn't mean you cannot scale the wall tomorrow; persistence is what makes success."

Gabriel "Sea Salt" Guerro

Gg

I AM...

Genius. Exceptional, intellectual, or creatively powerful or other natural ability.

Genuine. Truly what something is said to be; authentic.

Great. Measured to the extent, amount, or intensity considerably above the normal or average.

Graceful. Having or showing grace or elegance.

Generous. Showing a readiness to give more of something, as money or time, than is necessary or expected.

Growing. Becoming greater over a period of time; increasing.

Grounded. Well balanced and sensible.

Grateful. Feeling or showing an appreciation of kindness; thankful.

"What matters to an active man is to do the right thing; whether the right thing comes to pass should not bother him" Goethe

WHAT ARE YOU GRATEFUL FOR!

EXAMPLE: I am graceful with my approach.

"If you think you can or you
can't, you're right."
Henry Ford

Hh

I AM...

Harmonious. Forming a pleasing consistent whole.

Happy. Feeling or showing pleasure or contentment.

Hilarious. Extremely amusing.

Honest. Free of deceit and untruthfulness; sincere.

Humble. Showing a modest or low estimate of one's own importance.

Healthy. In good health.

"Optimism is the fruit that leads to achievement. Nothing can be done without hope and confidence." Helen Keller

HEALTHY SELF-TALK!

EXAMPLE: I am happy today!

"If I have seen further,
it is by standing on the
shoulders of giants."
Isaac Newton

Ti

I AM...

Incredible. Difficult to believe; extraordinary.

Intrepid. Fearless; adventurous.

Intelligent. Showing intelligence, especially of a high level.

Invincible. Too powerful to be defeated or overcome.

Indestructible. Not able to be destroyed.

Inspired. Brilliant or outstanding to a degree suggestive of divine inspiration.

"Look closely, the beautiful may be small"
Immanuel Kant

FUEL YOUR INSPIRATION!

EXAMPLE: I am intrepid in my pursuit of life!

"*Greatness and madness are next door neighbors; and they borrow each other's sugar.*"

Joe Rogan

I AM...

Jovial. Cheerful and friendly.

Judicious. Showing good judgment or sense.

Joyful. Feeling, expressing, or causing great pleasure and happiness.

Jubilant. Feeling or expressing great happiness and triumph.

Jaunty. Having or expressing a lively, cheerful, and self-confident manner.

Jocular. Fond of or characterized by joking; humorous or playful.

*"The shoe that fits one person pinches another; there is
no recipe for living that suits all cases."*
Carl Jung

EXPRESS YOUR JOY!

EXAMPLE: I am joyful for the success in my life!

"*My mojo so dope.*"
Kid Cudi

I AM...

Keen. Having or showing great perception or insight.

Kind-hearted. Having a kind and sympathetic nature.

Kingdom. The spiritual reign or authority of God.

Kudos. Praise and honor received for an achievement.

Kindness. The quality of being friendly, generous, and considerate.

King. A male sovereign or monarch; a man who holds by life tenure, and usually by hereditary right, the chief authority over a country and people.

"We have to continually be jumping off cliffs and developing our wings on the way down." Kurt Vonnegut.

SHARE YOUR KNOWLEDGE!

EXAMPLE: I am keen and see through to the end.

"Act well at the moment and you have performed a good action to all eternity."

Johann Kasper Lavater

I AM...

Light. The natural agent that stimulates sight and makes things visible.

Leader. The person who leads or commands a group, organization or country.

Liberty. Free to act as one pleases.

Loyal. Giving or showing firm and constant support or allegiance to a person or institution.

Lucky. Having, or bringing good luck.

Love. An intense feeling of deep affection.

"It's not the load that breaks you down, it's the way you carry it." Lena Horne

WHAT DO YOU LOVE?

EXAMPLE: I am loyal.

"Float like a butterfly,

sting like a bee."

Muhammed Ali

Mm

I AM...

Master. Having or showing very great skill or proficiency.

Mindful. Conscious or aware of something.

Moral. Holding or manifesting high principles for proper conduct.

Magnificent. Impressively beautiful, elaborate, extravagant, or striking.

Mettlesome. Full of spirit.

Maverick. An unorthodox or independent minded person.

"Live with no excuses and love with no regrets." <u>M</u>onel

WHAT COMES TO MIND?

Example: I am the master of my emotions.

"*Life shrinks or expands in proportion to one's courage.*"

Anais Nin

Nn

I AM...

Nirvana. (In Buddhism) A transcendent state which there is neither suffering, desire, non-sense of self, and the subject is released from the effects of karma and the cycle of death and rebirth. It represents the final goal in Buddhism.

Natural. A person regarded as having an innate gift or talent for a particular task or activity.

Noble. Having or showing fine personal qualities or high moral principles and ideals.

Now. Experiencing the present time or moment.

"That which does not kill us makes us stronger." Nietzsche

DO IT NOW!

EXAMPLE: I am noble in my actions.

"Lots of people want to ride with you in the limo, but what you want is someone who will take the bus with you when the limo breaks down."

Oprah Winfrey

I AM...

Original. The model or basis for imitations or copies.

Opportunity. The circumstance that makes it possible to do something.

Optimistic. Hopeful and confident about the future.

"Always forgive your enemies, nothing annoys them so much." <u>Oscar</u> Wilde

TAKE OWNERSHIP OF YOUR STRENGTHS!

EXAMPLE: I am optimistic about the opportunity!

"For a man to conquer himself is the finest and noblest of all victories."

Plato

I AM...

Patient. Able to accept or tolerate delays, problems, or suffering without becoming annoyed or anxious.

Peaceful. Free from disturbance; tranquil.

Positive. A good, affirmative, or constructive quality or attribute.

Prosperous. Bringing wealth and success.

Persistent. Continuing firmly or obstinately in a course of action in spite of difficulty an opposition.

Powerful. Having great power or strength.

"The world is changed by your example, not your opinion." Paulo Coelho

BE CREATIVE AND PLAYFUL!

EXAMPLE: I am prosperous!

"You have to stand for what you believe in and sometimes you have to stand alone."

Queen Latifah

I AM...

Quality. The standard of something as measured against other things of a similar kind, the degree of excellence of something.

Quintessential. Representing the most perfect or typical example of quality or class.

Questioner. A person who asks questions especially in an official context.

Quirky. Characterized by peculiar or unexpected traits.

Queenly. Fit for or appropriate to a queen.

"You have to know your real home is within."
Quincy Jones

WHAT ARE YOUR FAVORITE QUALITIES?

EXAMPLE: I am quintessential in this project!

"I don't stop when I'm tired.
I stop when I'm done."
Ragnar

Rr

I AM...

Responsible. Obligated to do something, or having control over or care for someone, as part of one's job or role.

Radiant. Clearly emanating great work, love or health.

Receptive. Willing to consider or accept suggestions and ideas.

Respectful. Feeling or showing deference and respect.

Rich. Plentiful; abundant.

Resolute. Admirably purposeful, determined and unwavering.

"The bond that links your true family is not one of blood, but of respect and joy in each other's life." Richard Bach

CREATE NEW RESOLUTIONS!

EXAMPLE: I am rich and radiant!

"A gem cannot be polished without friction, nor a man without trials."

Seneca

Ss

I AM...

Steady. Firmly fixed, supported or balanced; not shaking or moving.

Strategic. Designed with long-term overall aim and careful planning in order to achieve advantage.

Strong. Able to withstand great force or pressure.

Supportive. Providing encouragement or emotional help.

Successful. Accomplishing an aim or purpose.

Spirited. Full of energy, enthusiasm and determination.

Secure. Feeling safe, stable, and free from fear or anxiety.

"The problem is not the problem. The problem
is your attitude about the problem."
Captain Jack **S**parrow

LIST YOUR <u>S</u>TRENGTHS!

EXAMPLE: I am strong and successful!

"Believe you can,
and your halfway there."
Theodore Roosevelt

Tt

I AM...

Truthful. Telling or expressing the truth; honest.

Trustworthy. Able to be relied on as honest or truthful.

Tough. Able to endure hardship or pain.

Tranquil. Free from disturbance; calm.

Tenacious. Holding fast; characterized by keeping a firm hold.

Thankful. Expressing gratitude and relief.

"Our grand business is not to see what lies dimly at a distance, but to do what lies clearly at hand." Thomas Carlyle

TRUST YOURSELF!

EXAMPLE: I am thankful for the beauty in my life!

"He who takes responsibility for his life is the ruler of his destiny."

Unknown

Uu

I AM...

Unconditional. Not subject to any conditions.

Understanding. Capable of comprehending something.

Unflinching. Not showing fear or hesitation in the face of danger or difficulty.

United. Joined together politically for common purpose, or by common feelings.

Urbane. Courteous, and refined in manner.

Upbeat. Cheerful, positive and optimistic.

"Courage is looking fear in the eye and saying get out of my way I've got things to do." <u>Unknown</u>

ESTABLISH UPBEAT SELF-BELIEF!

EXAMPLE: I am unflinching in the face of adversity.

"To love and be loved is like feeling the sun from both sides."

David Viscott

I AM...

Virtuous. Having or showing high moral standard.

Vigorous. Strong, healthy, and full of energy.

Visionary. Thinking about or planning the future with imagination or wisdom.

Valued. Considered to be important or beneficial; cherished.

Vitality. Full of energy, the state of being strong, and active.

"Winners never quit, and quitters never win."
Vince Lombardi

WHAT ARE YOUR FAVORITE VALUES?

EXAMPLE: I am vigorous!

"Live passionately, even if it kills you because something is going to kill you anyway."
Webb Chiles

Ww

I AM...

Wise. Showing experience, knowledge, and good judgement.

Worthy. Showing the qualities or abilities that merit recognition in a specific way. Deserving effort, attention, respect.

Wealthy. Possessing a great deal of money, resources or assets; rich.

Winner. A person that wins.

Warrior. A person engaged in some struggle or conflict.

Well. Good or satisfactory in my ways.

"Do what you have to do, to do what you want to do." Denzel Washington

STATE YOUR <u>W</u>ISDOM!

EXAMPLE: I am worthy of self-love.

"Anything forced is not beautiful."

Xenophon

Xt

I AM...

Xenas. A tough, physical, confident woman.

Xenial. Being nice or friendly to foreign visitors.

Xenodochy. Receiving of strangers.

X-factor. Noteworthy quality or talent.

"Stumbling is not falling." Malcolm X

EXPRESS YOUR WISH!

EXAMPLE: I am xenodochy!

"Do. Or do not.
There is no try."
Yoda

I AM...

Yes. An affirmative reply.

Youthful. Experiencing the vitality or freshness of youth; vigorous.

Yearn. Experiencing an intense feeling of longing for something, typically something that one has lost or been separated from.

Yaba-daba-do. An expression of happiness or excitement.

Yay. Expressing triumph, approval, or encouragement.

"Train yourself to let go of everything you fear to lose." Yoda

WRITE ABOUT YOURSELF!

EXAMPLE: I am youthful in spirit!

"Live for who
and what you love."
Zayn Malik

Zz

I AM...

Zeal. Full of enthusiasm in pursuit of a cause or/an objective.

Zen. Experiencing a state of calm attentiveness.

Zest. Great enthusiasm and energy.

Zany. Amusingly unconventional and idiosyncratic.

Zealous. Full of, characterized by, or due to zeal. Ardently active, devoted, or diligent.

"Doing good to others is not a duty. It is a joy for it increases your own health and happiness." Zoroaster

ADD ZEST TO LIFE!

EXAMPLE: I am zealous!

A-Z

Poetry

POEMS
OF
TANNER HEIL

AWAKEN

Awaken
This is your mission
Arise
Manifest ultimate prize
Human
You were born to live and die
What will you do in life, what will you try?
Child of God
Seed of greatness
Awaken your spirit
Reach like a tree
To the sky
Into the ground
Let it be
Natural
Food, habits, drinks, sex
Grow
Release you necks
From the vice
From the yoke
Of meaningless direction
Life jokes
Ground your body
Humble your pride
Shed your geed
Release your lies
You are forgiven
Here is the fruit
Therein no sin
Only
Daily illusion suit.

BREATHE

What I want is pleasure
But how can you measure
The energy spent
Loving, giving, hustling hundred percent
Vital, vital, vital
Controlled idle
Tingle, ache, burn
It's your turn
Rise easy
Let it flow
Hold your keys
Let it go
Recycle that power
Truthfully build
Rise and fall, teach 'em skills
Breath in breath out
That's what it's all about!

CURVE BALL MOMENTS

Curve ball moments
Painted in our minds
Living breathing memories of time
Naked dancing wasted abstinence
Lively stories full of color and stance
Ocean waves
Sensations of crave
Feelings of distrust
Anger sadness lust
Let me go
The wind will blow
The fire will rage
And I like a bird will escape this cage.
Fully trapped, brain, body and rhyme
Caught in paranoia of sublime.
Free me God from my fear
Free your child from the year
Distortion, absence, delusion of presence.
In my mouth, I hunger
I reach, I desire
I inhale, I perspire
What is right?
What is wrong?
Do you know?
Your final act is just a show.
For yourself, for God.
Who will ever know the truth
In your mind
Only curve ball moments in time.

DANCING SUN

Smoke and mirrors
All but clear.
Illusion of time
Feather tail line
Fabric of space
Run your race
Spiritual dragon
Controlled Cannon.
Bold.
Cold.
Can you be?
As Gold as the sea
End of the day sun
The race is run
I pray
I adore
We Turn
Once more.
We rise
In the night
We see the bright
Sun
Who is never done.

ESSENTIALS

The ones who bleed,
All who speed
Racing to help with sirens a-blazing
Everyone saying
Who are the Essentials?
The essentials are
Ladies and men
Born of blood, bone, and skin
Faithfully growing
All born to win
To the end of the clock
We will never stop
We hammer and roar
The essentials give more.

FERN CREEK

We sat by the river
And it flowed
It poured
It rushed
It roared
Blue, emerald, green
Almost to chuckle mean
Leaves and roots
I sat on the rock
Wearing xtratuff boots
Sun rays sending down
Feeding the trees
Feeding the ground
We
Listen to the river sound.

GRIZZLY

Grizzly
January Sunset
Harbor light
Forever bright
Tough as the sea
Mariners around me
Dreaming dreaming
Grizzly
Furry mean bear
Deep inside you are soft and care
Damaged by the conditions
Working slaving mission
Grizzly
The Sun dawns
The waves break
Roll the dice chance fate
Fight like you do
Growl fierce and
Be you
Grizzly man.

HAMMER

Strike
Beat
Thump
Strike
Beat
Thump
Hammer
Hammer
Through the hump
Always hammer through
The mental stump.

INCH BY INCH

Inch by Inch
We get a mile
Me without you
Is a life without smiles
What would I do?
If zealot sank ship
What would I do?
Without your sweet lips
Deeper I dive, deeper I sink
Life is but a blink
Oh, you kill me
My mother told me of the sea
She said it is deep, bottomless and blue
Full figured – a beautiful woman, honest and true.

JUMP

Through our eyes
Fear controls our lives
Big or small
The concern is not the fall
The goal is to leap
It doesn't matter how steep
Just jump
It is only a hump
Be brave
Do not cave
For if you fall
You can always get back up
Regardless of success at all
It's about the courage to jump
With no fear at all.

KEYS TO THE KINGDOM

Ok ok I know it's time
I the avatar have awakened and enlivened
I the hobbit have walked the trail
I the thriving have come full circle
Understanding the sublime
The sun rises for you, shine!
The stars dance for you
The moon too!
Your favorite brassicas meant to eat
Sustaining energy, head to feet
Quinoa, farro, apples, and salmon
Divinely designed
Man and woman
Vibrational waves enter my ears
Symbols, sign, code message for years
Straighten your spine
Relax, let go,
Feel the rhythm feel the flow
Be the creator of your mind
You are the guardian
You hold the keys
Change the story, the script you see
Interconnected and woven
Time and space, your seed egg chosen
Peace welcomes and embraces
You are hero of ten thousand faces
Masked, robed, and ready to fight
Humble, warrior powerful sight
Looking into the future
Looking into the blue
Experiencing you.
May the dawning of day
Be exactly as you wish
Serendipitous.

LIGHT GRID

Light grid
All of gold
Washing cleansing
Yellow and bold
Light grid
Beaming on me
Sharing life eternally
Golden rays emanating
Soulful joy radiating
Pain, sorrow, grief
Golden belief
Pierced and broken
The higher power has spoken
You bleed love, the color
White full of light
Imagine
Flying soaring graceful wings
Graceful divine sentient being
Light grid
God of gold
Return the freedom, restore the bold
Fuel your patrons, feed your kin
Rejuvenate the American

MOMENTO MORI

Looking at dead people
Pictures lost with time
Forgotten and wasted
Moments and sighs
My old self sits there
With my grandpa that once stood
A man taller than I
A man I knew as good
I didn't know then
He was to leave so soon
I didn't know how to make room
For myself and him
I would give anything to see again.
I contemplate my journey and walk away
From everything I love and play
There is a voice inside my head
A whisper that can only come from the dead
Your time will come
When all is done
And your time to fly
Like an eagle in the sky
Have no fear
Be courageous
Expect Outrageous
Act with intention
Go outside and listen
Soak up the sun
Dance and have fun
Drink the wine
Kill some time
Lick the sweetness
From the fruit
Try it all, wear the suit

Remember to splash
And let life splash you
Be prepared to be surprised
Open your eyes and live alive
you are perfectly prepared
To be you
Nothing is better than acting true.

NIGHT

Yup me
One more time,
I dare you
Ill stare right through you
Into my own right,
Black as night
Ill slow down my role
Magnetic like the poles
Polar opposites
Edgy and serrated I slit
I'll slow down my speed
I'll be like the seasons
Wintered and freed
Cold and frozen
Ready to be released
Ready to be new
Time began falling with you
When the wind between us
Was silent.

OCTAGON SECRETS

The antidote
The cure
Has been wrote
To wipe clean
The addiction feen.
The antidote has been found
Deep in the earth
Deep in the ground
Mysteriously the secret has always been around
Follow the map and you will find
Treasure and abundance in time
You must find a spot and sit down
Take a breath make some sound
Feel your heart beating inside
Imagine and visualize
The blood flowing
The continuous pump
The autonomic system
Failing to give up.

POWER OF THE BRAIN

Be wild and jump in
You too can be tough as them
You got to train
In the heat, snow and rain
You can completely rewire
And live inspired
Does your brain feel alive?
Mine is buzzing like a beehive
My body is charged
And my spirit enlarged
I let the energy flow
From head to toe
The atoms vibrate through life
Bouncing, bumping
Day and night.
Be wild and jump in
That's what it takes to win.

QUALITY

Do it right
Be clean and tight
Be cautious, take a breath
Think it through
Right to tighten
Left to loosen
Pursuit of excellence
Order of importance
Steps to be taken
Mechanics never forsaken.

RUSH

I stood there
Flooded wet soaked
Tall straight and erect
Arms together hands clasped
Stretched to the sky
Naked, showering cold
Euphoric gold
Invigorating rush
Tighten core – retain the heat
Breathe smooth and deep
Pain release
Mind over matter
I stand the test
Controlled willpower
Seeking peace and rest.

SEAMEN

The bird said "Hey
Fuck you man
I'm over it
And ready to go back to land."
The salt hung heavy to his bottom lip
Wind burned, and thirsty for a drink
Hustled by the boss of the sea
We pushed pots uphill
Against the waves and swell
110lb maneaters
Loaded to catch crustacean creatures
The trip was short
Only a month worth of work
We brailed with red solo cups
Focsle wet feeling like hells lair
Without a shower matted hair
We bucked 30 knot wind and sea
Reaching the limit of what we can be
It was Christmas day
Pushing our mariner's way
Peanut butter sandwiches and nature valley
Not a normal holiday
We missed our ladies
We missed our friends
We missed our family
Then again, we were seaman.

TOOTH BRUSH

Tooth brush toothpaste on the ground
Dead and silent with no sound
Screaming attention pick me up
Put me where I belong in my cup
No attention no care
No worry no fear
College student, busy life
One shot, two shot party knife
No fucks given leave a mess
Moms not home got no stress
Raging impatience frustrated core
Where's my toothpaste?
On the floor
Forgotten, kicked, neglected and left
Wasteful choices, lazy craft
Change your sheets, make your bed
Clear the toxic, clear your head
Breath of life for us all
When you drop the stress and start small
Home, head, body, world
Release the dragon, wings unfurled
Heavenly relief to mankind
Open the gates to sunshine
Maybe there you can see
Your toothpaste, your responsibility.

ULTIMATE PRIZE

Healthy wealthy and wise
Swagger Winner Prize
Impenetrable soul
Radiate heart love gold
Emergence phoenix have true courage
Roar lion release imaginary bondage
Liberty, life, love
Welcome you from above
Bright sunshine, opposite dark night
Work together to balance universal might
Birthed catalyst, encourage truth
Fire burning, raging Invictus proof
Healthy wealthy wise
Pillars of independence, victories surprise
Humanity rejoice, humanity reclaim
Release internal negative pain
Timing is perfect here's your gain
Live, listen, see and grow
Even you
Begin now, go!

VICTORY

I woke up this morning with a smile on my face
Finally realizing how to win this grand ole' race
I've been dancing with the devil, smoking with the lord
Sleeping in till 3 and breaking up because I was bored
I've gone crazy wondering when it's all going to change
I read a book today about the wild and strange
More confused than ever I surrendered today
I'm just a soul that needs to party and play
I traveled the world, went from sky bars in Bangkok
To marble pillars in Athens and thought about this spinning rock
Smoked herb in coffee shops from Amsterdam
Feeling so high
I felt like Jesus man
A monster told me to quit my job
I laughed and told them to chew on their cob
This world needs more lovers. The world needs more saints
Live now! Don't wait
Come on warrior now drink the grapes of life
Fight the monsters, conquer strife
It's time to pick up your ideas and mind
No more sorrow no more fear
Have 2020 vision no matter what year
Shed your burdens, find your pride
Lose the anger, kill the lies
Realize the power inside your great mind
Find the light within your heart
It's the only place to start
You are the brave unconquerable soul
You are Invictus leader visionary bold
Zen excelsior nirvana - welcome back Americana
Passionate humble spirit, I see you flying high
Break the chains and speak your mind
It's time to realize we are more than rich

Question all, trust few, seal your lips
Alpha and Omega Kingdom, scars and stitch
You are special, the one and only you.
Knowledge is power, here's my truth
Death is stalking, life is loose
Laugh, be happy, hold your lover close
Smile child, my dear friend
This is the end.

WORKING MAN

Can you work and stay steady?
Can you be defeated, and weary?
Can you keep your head up and level?
Can you let go and believe in revel?
Can you listen and not talk back?
Can you give everything you have and still attack?
Knowing it's all going to change,
Crossing mountains and range.
Can you say please?
Can you give relieve?
Are you fit for life of men?
And gentle to women?

XTRA TOUGH

Siracha
Rubber bands
Tiger balm
Brown boots
Wet head, wet hands
Who's selling out today?
Who's pushing the way?
Zip ties
Siracha
Rubber bands
Tiger balm
Ocean swell
Fisherman's

Coffee coffee
Oh, so sweet
You help me move my feet
Captains charging
Bearing down
Surrender all
Surrender crown
Take up the thorns
of sacrifice
Hold your head high
Bear the knife
Who's selling out today?
Who's willing to work for play?
Who's singing the workers song?
Who's going the mile long?
Zip ties
Siracha
Rubber bands
Brown boots
Tiger balm
Brute fisherman.

YOU

Lyrical violence forged in time
Lyrical violence holding sign
The rhythm rolls and the music stops
You were a king amongst the skulls and rocks
You were meant to rise upon the tide
You were meant to ride and die
A collapse in final victory
Silence of eternity
Victory won
Hero song sung
All cheer your name
You will be remembered
Welcome to the hall of fame
You have won
You found the peace
You settled the war
You mastermind the story
You recreated and prayed holy
Nothing would stop you not even the rain
You took responsibility, knowing you would be to blame
You Hustled and slaved
You labored and paid
In sweat
In blood
In effort life and love
Giving it all for a dream
Sell out now, give all steam
The rivers been flowing
Your senses are alive
Your vertebrates are dancing
Your souls divine
Awakened by now
Seeing through the illusion
Triumphant energy fusion.

ZEALOT CHILD

Be free my child
And hold your smile
To the sky
Be free my child
Speak no lies
Be free my child
I know your stress
I've been dancing too
With the test
Be free my child
I understand your pain
I've been stuck inside my brain
Be free my child
Let it go
Enjoy life and watch it grow.

ABOUT THE AUTHOR

Tanner Heil is an athlete and entrepreneur. He is an active human who enjoys the outdoors. He loves to explore and experience nature. His hobbies include smoking fish, mountain biking, and strumming his guitar. He loves to read and soak up the sun. Tanner is passionate about life and loves planet earth. He is a devoted and faithful family man. He shares his time home with his beautiful wife Abigail. Together they manifest happiness in their home with the dog Roxy, and cats Badger and Blossom.

Printed in the United States
by Baker & Taylor Publisher Services